Paul
Don't ever give
up on your Dreams!

CW01572602

2013

Dear Tony

Sue Selfe

Design and editing by Sandy Newberg, Baileymarkham Design,
www.baileymarkham.com

Front and back cover photo inserts by John Selfe

Photo acknowledgements
Page 8, Henry Grossman
Page 40, Tribune Photos
Page 54, Tom Hutsler
Page 64, Jay Bernstein

ISBN 978-0-9574068-2-7
Stagedoor Publishing

Contents

The book is dedicated to my son
Daniel John Selfe
The man who still makes me laugh

I don't know why I decided to write this book now. I do know as I sat in front of the computer the words seemed to write themselves. I passed each draft to old and a few new friends for their opinions, and when I few called me and sounded choked I knew I had got it right.

Over the many years that have passed since Tony left me I question how anyone gets over this man. I guess the answer is you don't. So you bounce around and create projects so the world can again remember his magic and joy.

I bounce around, I don't want to forget the impact he has had on my life. I don't want to forget that I was once loved by this giant of a man.

Newley lovers are special people and over the years I have met some gems, so let me thank you.
Jenny and David Bemmer, my oldest friends and confidants
Graham and Shazzie Brill for believing in me
Andrea Kohlegger for her vision, support, and love
Sandy Newberg for…this page is not long enough
Toby Strain for sharing my dreams
Paul Goodhead for still trying to understand me
Tammy, Carrie, and Daniel Selfe for standing by their crazy mother
Kacey and Jayden because I love them
John Selfe for loving me when many a man wouldn't, and because I love him so very, very much.
Danny Greenstone for calling me a writer and a creative
Barbara Angela Kealey for making me laugh
Lee Edward Bartlett for helping to create Newley Night
Jeannette and Ronald Newman the greatest of the great
Vera and William Selfe for John
Anthony George Newley for showing me beauty in everything I see and do, I will always love you!
Why would you want to forget someone who gave you so much to remember, you wouldn't, would you?
Enjoy
Suzie xx

This is a love story.

How do you define love?

For this story, I would say that "love is the unselfish, loyal, and benevolent concern for the good of another."

In the space of a few months, I went from Barbie dolls to Broadway, from innocence to something I never expected to happen in a million years.

The man I am writing about deserves to shine on these pages, and I will try my best to ensure that this happens.

I hope by the end of this book you will agree that:
"Love Has The Longest Memory Of All" — Anthony George Newley

This is my story.

Neon Glow

I fell in love with you as the sun dipped so low,
in the middle of Soho amid a neon glow.
A girl so young and an older man took a risky journey,
and walked it hand in hand.
Don't cry, Flower, you whispered as you wiped my tears away,
Tomorrow you will smile as tomorrow is our day.
The days became months, and the months became years,
We became one, there were doubts, there were fears.
Those days are long gone, but my love still remains.
I still feel the joy, I still feel the pain.
I remember that night as the sun dipped so low,
I fell in love with you, Tony, amid a neon glow.

Susan Jane Selfe   September 2013

'The Roar's' A Whisper

By JOHN McCLAIN
Drama Critic

THE REPORT on "The Roar of the Greasepaint—and The Smell of the Crowd" has to be a sort of weaseling thing from this quarter, because I think the music is magical a lot of the time and I have the fanciest respect for both Anthony Newley and Cyril Ritchard, but I cannot say with honesty that the little fantasy in which they are involved makes the grade.

The stage is set in a series of circular platform, and in the center is a circular board, marked off numerically like a roulette table, and the game is a contest between Ritchard, who re-presents The Establishment, or privilege, or something, and Mr. Newley, who is the Common Man. There is a Greek chorus of little urchins who sing and scamper around in the background, striking poses and draping themselves from ladder-like props, and they are extremely effective and active.

theme is ephemeral, and it is a bit much to rely upon the two principals to carry the entire proceedings on their gifted shoulders.

"THE ROAR OF THE GREASEPAINT— THE SMELL OF THE CROWD," at the Sam S. Shubert Theatre. Pre-sented by David Merrick in associa-tion with Bernard Delfont. Book, music and lyrics by Leslie Bricusse and Anthony Newley. Production de-signed and lighted by Sean Kenny. Costumes by Freddy Wittop. Musical direction Herbert Grossman. Orches-trations by Philip J. Lang. Vocal and dance music arranged by Peter How-ard. Musical numbers staged by Gil-lian Lynne. Associate Producer Samuel Liff. Directed by Mr. Newley.

THE CAST

Sir	Anthony Newley
Cocky	Cyril Ritchard
The Kid	Sally Smith
The Girl	Joyce Jillson
The Negro	Gilbert Price
The Bully	Murray Tannenbaum

THIS MR. NEWLEY is a superb performer, as well as being responsible with Leslie Bricusse for the book, music and lyrics, and there is just no way for Mr. Ritchard to be less than captivating. But the game they are playing becomes tedious as the even-ing wears on, I thought, tedious and rather remote, not going anywhere in parti-cular despite a lot of. sym-bolic talk. We have had the social consciousness stuff up to here.

The good things about the show are the music and the dancing. The record is al-ready being played around town, and most of us have heard "Who Can I Turn To" and "Things To Remember," but there is a particular thrill in seeing them dished up by Mr. Newley and Mr. Ritchard in the flesh, with the aid of the strange assortment of squalid little boys and girls, who comprise the chorus. Gillian Lynne has done a magnificent job with the choreography.

My parents' clipping of the review from THE ROAR OF THE GREASEPAINT — THE SMELL OF THE CROWD

Dear Tony

Chapter One

Letter to My Love

June 1965

Dear Mr. Newley,

My name is Susan Newman and I came to see you on Broadway last night. I was not meant to come, only there was nobody to watch me. Oh, I am 9 years old.

I was all dressed up. I wore my best blue satin dress. The lady I was sitting next to smelt of tobacco and milk duds and said how pretty I looked.

I was told not to talk, not to go to the bathroom, or not to fidget. I did none of that, Mr. Newley, as I thought you were wonderful. I didn't like Sir, and the way he treated you. It was a bad game he played. I knew by your face how hurt you were and I wanted to hug you so bad. When you fell to your knees in front of me and sang to God, I cried, but quietly so nobody knew.

This was my first time at the theatre, and you are now my favourite singer in all the world. I liked the show and you very much. I will write again on pretty flower paper.

Goodbye Mr Newley and thank you,

Love,

Susan x

September 1965

Dear Mr Newley,

Thank you for writing back, and I will call you Tony the next time.

I keep listening to *Roar of the Greasepaint*, and guess what, I have *Stop the World*, too. My dad gave it to me. I never saw that one as I was even younger then, but I love the music and some of the songs made me laugh. I love clowns and your picture in makeup is very nice.

My dad said you are from England. He is too. I like it there very much. My Grandma lives there.

Do you know the Queen? Does she like your singing too?

My cousins keep laughing at me because I listen to your music. I like the Beatles (they are English too), but I have never seen them, but I have you.

I don't care what they say. There is another record I saw in the window of the store and I may get that soon if I'm good. I do hope I get to see you sing again someday.

My dad said you are a good actor too and he said I can watch you on TV if something comes on. I hope it is on early so I can stay up.

Goodbye Mr. Newley, if I like the new record I may write again.

Love,

Susan Newman x

So Brooklyn remained the same, The trains still ran on the EL, the horns still beeped constantly, Young's bar on the corner replaced their window every Monday, because every Saturday night someone came shooting through it. Pop's candy store still made the best egg cream, and I continued to absorb and learn about the magic of Newley.

The TV Guide was like a bible, I would read every little thing to see if Newley was on a show, it was exciting really.

Life was more than okay on Palmetto Street. I lived on the third floor of a brownstone Number 1712, I will never forget that number.

I would sit by the window every afternoon and wait for my father's return from Schaefer's Brewery. I never had many friends, and my cousin Regina who lived down the street was like a little sister to me.

My parents adored me and I was wrapped in more cotton wool than the druggist could keep in stock.

Our landlady was quite stern. She spent every day scrubbing the stoop (these were the stone steps that led up to the communal front door), only for little Stevie Champullion

10

Dear Tony

on the ground floor to drop his Italian ice on them. We all watched, transfixed, as the multitude of ants appeared within seconds to lap up the sticky, sweet liquid, followed closely by Mrs. Giel chasing us away with her mop.

My landlord's family were circus people and they spent the whole summer in Sarasota. I loved hearing their stories and they would invite us in to see home movies. The flickering light from the projector and the sound of the film as it went through the reel always caused great excitement. We would sit and eat popcorn, I loved it!

I did hear my dad say on more than one occasion, "You've seen one circus, you've seen them all!" Mom would shrug and we would always go again.

I adored clowns from a very early age, when most children were frightened, I just lapped them up. My claim to fame? I starred on Bozo the Clown's TV show three times. Did you hear me? Three times!

The Giels' daughter Joanie was older than me, but we were both very shy and we hit it off. We would go down in the basement and she would tell stories of her family; they were trapeze artists and became quite famous as I recall, they played Circus, Circus in Vegas.

I would play Newley and sing and dance. In many ways we were connected, and in latter years the connection would become clearer.

Palmetto street was full of eccentrics, and great community camaraderie. Neighbours fought one minute and then married the next. There was a laundromat on one corner owned by an odd lady whose dog was as big as a horse — odd because the dog was a St. Bernard whose name was Trigger. Across the street was a little restaurant, but people didn't go there to eat; Dad said it was a drug den. I ate a couple of hot dogs there once and the only "high" I got was from too much Pepto Bismol.

I had a crush on a nice boy, Pee Wee Pollack. He lived above the little restaurant. Another little chap, but my feelings changed, too, after having seen "Roar."

Funny how one event can change your life so drastically.

My parents brought me into an amazing family. Family was important then. I had a huge extended family, and I loved them all.

My weekends were spent sitting on the fire escape. That was my palace, my jungle, my Shangri-La. It was, in fact, anything I wanted it to be. I would have lunch out there and sit for hours writing. I always loved writing. My mom would give me a jug of iced tea. How come no one makes iced tea like your mom used to?

On really hot New York days, Tommy (I can't remember his last name) would loosen the cap on the fire hydrant. Gosh, what a treat to be cool! We dodged in and out of the cars, the buses, and our mothers' smacks. We seemed so innocent then, thrilled by simple things.

I think I'm still thrilled at simple things and every day to me is an adventure. I believe I can thank our dear friend for giving me that gift.

I didn't tell you about Joanie's uncle, Uncle Herbert. He was very cool and always dressed as a clown. Uncle Herbert would stand in the vestibule wearing his red nose and honk it whenever we entered. Let's face it, as a kid you think everything is cool. I didn't realize the poor man had a problem. Now, all these years later, "Why can't I cast away this mask of play?" springs to mind!

The record player my Uncle Harry and Aunt Evie bought me was in continuous use. My mom bought me the album called *Who Can I Turn To?*

I soon added more to my ever-growing collection. *Newley Recorded, Newley Delivered*, and I played "Pop Goes The Weasel" over and over.

Christmas in New York was approaching. What is it they say about America, we always do it bigger and better? Well, with Christmas, there is no argument from me. Santa stood on every street corner, Fat and jolly, thin and miserable, and some who really should have never gotten the damn job. The shop windows were always the most fascinating; everything seemed to shine and move. I knew at a very young age just how blessed I was to be born in New York. "Greatest city in the world," you could hear someone utter those words on a daily basis, I believed it to be true. I guess even now, deep down in my heart, she still has her place. It was a shame I left her so soon.

So off we went to Radio City Music Hall. This was the place dreams came true. I used to sit and watch the beautiful Rockettes, every step and kick timed to perfection, on this occasion they were all dressed in red and green velvet. There was a choir too and every note was sung on key. It was an exciting time, but it was going to get even better.

Anthony Newley was in the film we were going to see, a whole film with him in it. There were advertisements in all the papers. My dad would shout, as everyday I would cut out the advertisements before he had a chance to read it. The poster of Doctor Dolittle riding a giraffe was amazing, the model of a a big pink snail filled the lobby, and the words "starring Anthony Newley" could be clearly seen.

My mom bought me a paper doll book, I had it for years and only recently passed it on to a dear friend.

Dear Tony

I could not sleep the night before, the hell with visions of sugar plums dancing in my head. I had my Cocky, Littlechap and that bloody weasel popped more times than I care to remember. I got dressed in my finest red velvet pants and wore my new pink Nehru jumper, he couldn't see me, but boy, did I notice him!

December 1967

Dear Tony,

How are you? It's me Susan Newman, I hope you remember me.

I just saw *Doctor Doolittle* and I loved it. I've got a book of paper dolls. It doesn't look like you, but it is very nice. You looked so cute (I hope it is okay to say that) and I loved the clothes you wore. Did you like all the animals? To think you worked with Mr. Rex Harrison. You must have been so happy! Do you know what my mom said? "Mr Sexy Rexy". <3

I saw the movie in Manhattan, but Mom said if it comes to the RKO in Ridgewood, she will take me again.

I did an essay in English about Doctor Doolittle, I got a B. I think I should have spoken more about the film than Matthew Mugg.

Mr. Newley (Tony), may I have a signed picture please? I will hang it next to my picture of Davy Jones.

Goodbye, Tony. I can't wait for your next film, you are still my favourite.

Love,

Susan x

Palmetto Street, Brooklyn, New York

Ronald and Jeannette Newman, March 1944

Dear Tony

Chapter Two

The Father of This Girl

The films did come and my life would change forever.

My parents can only possible be described by me as near darn perfect. They were married 14 years before I was born. Dad had malaria during the war that affected his fertility, and they were told after many tests that with different partners a baby might have been possible, but together a no-go! So, when I showed up on 14 February 1956, I could have not have been more loved and welcomed.

So of course I was brought up on my parents' music. Sinatra, Darren, Martin, Davis and Garland, Washington, Starr, and my beautiful Newley.

The house was always filled with show tunes. My parents would sing to each other, they would jokingly say they were Jeanette Macdonald (my mom was called Jeannette) and my dad was Nelson Eddy. "I Am Calling Youuuu!" Dad would sing, and Mom knew he wanted tea.

It's hard getting the parenting thing right. I know that now, but they were wonderful, like the greatest double act.

My dad was a great mimic. I loved his Charles Laughton impression, and he could do Newley's "Pop Goes The Weasel." At family parties dad would always sing "I'm Enery the Eighth I am" in his strongest Cockney accent. Yes, Palmetto street was a happy place then.

Here is love story one.

My father was a British Navy frogman whose ship grounded in Coney Island in 1942. My mom was with her siblings (there were eight) but five of them were out that night. My mother was beautiful, with long raven black hair and those beautiful brown "come to bed eyes." My dad approached her and asked her for a dime to use the phone. My father was a handsome man, and in his uniform he could have easily been a Hollywood movie star.

They fell in love that very moment, as the story goes. I believe it because when the ship finally left two days later, Dad jumped off to get back to her and ended up in jail. On his release from the British Navy, they married. They were a beautiful couple, and I grew up with love, laughter, and a humour to surpass the finest comedies. My dad decided to make America his home after he met my mom. He also wanted to become an American citizen and told me how my mother would sit with him for hours and teach him American history. He so fell in love with America right after he so fell in love with my mom. He was so proud the first time he pledged his allegiance. They were some team, I was glad to be part of it!

I always lived on Palmetto Street, and the house was filled with music. show tunes, classical, and jazz. I would dance in front of my parents as soon as I could walk. I would put on shows for my dolls and stuffed toys. I was going to go to drama school. I was going to be something special.

I remember when the Oscars were on I was allowed to stay up late, I always had a new nightgown for the occasion. Mom and I would sit and watch from start to finish. When it finished it was our turn. And the winner for best daughter is Susan Jane Newman! The winner for the best mother in the world Jeannette Newman! How excited we were when *Doctor Doolittle* won for best song!

We had a nice apartment with railroad rooms. We lived under the El. I would tell my cousins I controlled the trains that ran outside the window. I knew when they were arriving, and would push the button on the vacuum cleaner and they believed me as the train sped past.

We had pretty furniture, too — Art Deco. How I would love that pink and mint green sofa now. When I think back and see my parents sitting on it, they could have stepped out of any 1960s sitcom. They were a beautiful couple. The Lucy and Desi of Palmetto Street.

We traveled to England every other summer and saw my grandparents. Life was wonderful. My grandparents loved me to visit too. 59 Glenhurst Road in Brentford was always important to me and would become even more so later in my life.

1968

Dear Tony,

I nearly wrote Charlie. *Sweet November* was wonderful, You looked beautiful too!

My friend Debbie went with me, she didn't like it at all. Please don't get mad at me, but I did not like Sandy Dennis. She is a good actress. I liked her in *Up The Down Staircase,* but

I could have chosen a better Sara for you. Why didn't she want to love you? You would have really cared for her, and loved her. Oh, how I want to see this film again.

I so love you! I'm sorry! First time I have said that. My face is red!

I did cry when you had to walk out that door into the cold.

I know I don't really love you, but my heart pounds when I see you on the television too. My first crush, Mom says.

We walked over Brooklyn Bridge today, I wanted to be Sara Deever just for a little while. We had hot dogs too, no sauerkraut. "How Sweet It Is."

I can't wait for your next role, I hope it is something wonderful and one you will be happy in. Please fall in love with someone who will love you back next time.

I must tell you, I have skipped a grade in school. I am hoping to be in drama school soon.

Goodbye Tony, if you can send another picture that would be nice.

Love,

Susan X

Dear Tony,

Thank you for the lovely picture, it did make me laugh. You can really pull some funny faces. Do you often ride a bike?

I bet you have a real nice car. My uncle Harry just bought a new Caddy, really nice. What do you drive?

I will be auditioning for the school play soon. I wish I could sing like you, but no one can sing like you.

I heard another singer today sing "Who Can I Turn To?" He was good, but even mom said Tony Bennett is no Anthony Newley, I agree! I bought a magazine and you were in it, I will keep it with all my other souvenirs of you. I have many nice things now. I won't ask, but if ever you want to send me another picture, I would love that.

I bought a red frame for my "Matthew" picture. It looks so nice.

Hope we talk again soon,

Dear Tony

Goodbye Tony,

Love,

Susan x

We had a holiday in England again this year! I enjoyed our usual sightseeing days. The record stores in England are so cool and you can listen before you buy. So much Newley too, I bought two albums, and an EP, looks like a single, but better!

There were pictures of Anthony Newley in most of the windows. I even asked dad to take a picture.

My cousin Linda, seven years older than me and beautiful with her blonde beehive and thick black mascara, offered to take me to the "Cinema", she was going to surprise me. SURPRISE me! I nearly died! An x-rated film with Mr. Newley! Oooooh! I dressed "posh" and got in to the theater with no bother.

1969

Dear Tony,

Heironymus Merkin. Wow. I know I shouldn't have seen it, but my cousin Linda took me when I was in London. I have gotten really tall so just walked in. You did look happy in this film. I didn't understand the whole thing, but the bits I understood were great! My cousin said it was your life story, but I am sure that is not like you. I loved the character though, very much! In this film you did get the girls, and they sure loved you back!

My first kind of adults-only film. My parents don't know, but they have enough to worry about.

You are so handsome! Your family is beautiful, I saw you on *Hollywood Palace,* too. How lovely to see your little girl. My mother thinks that was your mother in the audience, how very proud everyone must be of you. I recognised all the songs, so beautiful. Will you do any more shows like that, any in Brooklyn so I can come?

Now back to *Heironymus.* I adored it. Your wife is so beautiful, I would love to look like her. I have a kaftan mom bought me, I wanted one like the one you wore in the film. They are hard to get, but I still feel quite special when I wear it. Mine is blue and covered in flowers.

I loved the songs especially "I'm All I Need," Sad, but very pretty.

I'm sorry I haven't written to you for a long time, my dad is very sick. He had a heart attack and I have been so sad. Sometimes I find it hard to listen to the music. My mom is sad too. I'm hoping he will feel better soon and we can all share your music and some laughter again.

Thank you for the picture of Charlie. It is hanging above my bed (I took Davy Jones down!)

A *Merkin* picture would be nice to add to my collection!

Goodbye Tony,

I'll write again soon, You are wonderful.

Love,

Susan X

Late 1960s

So the music stopped for quite a while.

My dad stayed in hospital, my mom cried, and I spent more time in the basement with Joanie. What excited me more than anything was that Joanie's folks saw Anthony Newley in Las Vegas and even gave me a picture they took of him on stage. I longed to go and see him there one day.

I couldn't go to drama school as my poor dad had to give up work. My dear mother had been doing a few shifts at National shoes on Myrtle Avenue. Dad hated her working there, but he didn't know.

I wasn't doing too well at school, I couldn't concentrate. I resolved to try harder as I wanted to go to drama school one day, and the tuition was expensive. I wanted to get a good job and help my parents. I wanted to be something, whatever that something is.

I know Dad compared me all the time to my cousin. He didn't mean to hurt me, but it did. She finished high school at 16. I know things about her I promised I would never tell, I think I will always do my best, but I want to be me.

I joined the drama club in school. I loved it. Mr. Fury, my drama teacher, was a small man with a mass of thick red hair and a matching moustache. He did this kind of scene where he wrapped his arms around himself and made it look like he was dancing with a woman.

It was a dance scene from a film called *Top Hat,* so clever. I did my scene from *West Side Story,* I was good. Maybe one day, I thought, I will be an actress, or a dancer.

Mr. Fury liked it and said I was a natural. I starred in *Bye Bye Birdie* as Mrs McAfee, I wondered if my parents would be able to come? Drama seems to be all I care about, but I am in the glee club too. So there are a few subjects I enjoy, which is good.

I remember a day when I went sick. I told my mom a white lie. I saw in the *TV Guide* that Anthony Newley was on *Merv Griffin.* I needed to smile and it worked.

That voice, I just love listening to him sing. There is no one like him, there never will be. I put a record on later that day and I felt lighter. "I'll do it my way or not at all" kept playing in my head. "Dream…I had this wonderful dream where I fight and I kill every dragon in sight." I lay on the couch and fell asleep. I dreamt of being on a big stage and dancing. People cheered and everyone was so proud. "Pity, it's only a dream!"

I made up my mind I would try really hard to do better in school and not be so sad all the time. I scheduled an appointment with guidance counsellor Dr. Gerber, I needed someone to talk to. I am afraid to upset my mom. The thought of losing either one of my parents scares me so.

I started a course on Hitchcock and enjoyed the many films I got to see. Mom had never seen *Psycho* and I knew she would love it. One night we stayed up really late and watched it. She seemed happier and I so enjoyed a little quality time with her. That was the last time in a long time that would happen.

Dad was released from hospital. He wasn't happy anymore and no matter what Mom did seemed to be wrong. He was different, he was grumpy all the time. Mom said he had to adjust, we all had to adjust. Music that gave him such great pleasure just annoyed him now.

The words "don't upset your father" constantly rang in my ears.

Dad slept a lot, and when he was awake I had to be quiet. I asked Joanie if I wanted to play music could I sit in the basement? So just me, the garbage cans, the odd water bug and Newley.

Dear Tony,

I hope you are happy. I hope soon to be happy again soon.

I have the new LP I love it. So now you have a moustache.

Is it for a new film? I can only imagine that it why you grew it.

You look different. My mother laughed when she saw the cover. "Why did he do that?" I like it, I guess because I like you so much!

Saw you on TV a few times, you are really funny.

I'm doing really good in school.

Things are still difficult at home, but dad is looking better. I play music in my bedroom again, just very low.

I like a song in the charts, "Close to You" by the Carpenters. Do you know Burt Bacharach? I like his songs,very cool. Not like I like yours and Mr Bricusse. I cannot ever imagine liking anyone as much as you two..

Tony, can I have a picture of you with the moustache?

My friend's parents saw you in Vegas again. They said you were the best singer they ever saw. I even lent them an LP. Everyone loves you, especially me!

I'll write again soon,

Goodbye Tony,

Love,

Sue xxx

Picture sent to me; Tony filming the original 1968 version of SWEET NOVEMBER,
signed later

Dear Tony

Chapter Three

At the Crossroads

1970s

My dad's health continued to deteriorate.

I was getting ready to sit exams and studied really hard.

We put on *South Pacific*. It really was a great show. I was in the chorus and my friend Diane Patterson played Bloody Mary. I didn't mind that my parents could not come. I didn't cry because they missed the play. I think I cried enough in the previous days because this would probably be my last school production.

Barbara managed to get us tickets for the *Concert for Bangladesh* as a goodbye gift (I'll explain soon).

Oh, what a day! The stage was filled with great stars. I never thought I'd see George Harrison, Dylan, Billy Preston, and CLAPTON, who I fell in love with that day. I dressed like him, with velvet blazers and grandad shirts and my long brown hair was now curly.

I went and bought a few LPs and raved continually about what I had experienced that day. Money continued to be a problem, but when I came home from school on Tuesday, my parents had bought me the album. It was a double set and I knew it was expensive. I listened a little and then bound it with the finest red ribbon to pack.

I didn't write to Tony, because somehow it didn't seem right. I told him no one would ever take his place and here I was in love with a rock star. I told Dr Gerber. I bet he thought I was mad.

"Susan, you will fall in love a thousand times before you find Mr. Right." Oh, Dr. Gerber, all those degrees sir, and you still got it wrong!

That phone call came just before dinner, a week before the school play. It was Uncle George, who lived next door to my grandma in England. He was sick, had cancer and Grandma was becoming old and confused and they could not manage. My dad was in turmoil as he could not fly. His health was still bad and the doctor said absolutely not.

"Sue, you will have to go, I have nobody else to ask."

I loved England. All my holidays were spent there. From Brooklyn to Brentford used to thrill me, but now I was filled with dread.

I would finish school in England. There was an American school and they agreed to take me under the difficult circumstances.

My mom bought me a proper trunk, black and white with little drawers. I thought a suitcase would be better. I mean, how long was I going for? The trunk would be sent by boat as it was far too expensive for air mail. I put in all the things I had on my dresser. My special things…my doll of Queen Elizabeth, My wishnicks, my black light posters, my patchouli oil, a few of those glass ornaments of animals with great big sad eyes, etc.

I would have to wait for all my things to get there. So I took the old blue suitcase and packed what I really wanted. Newley came with me, I knew there would be little else to bring me comfort.

I was given a party the night before I left. I tell you with hand on heart I don't remember anything, not a thing! The only thing I remember is finding one of my Aunt Rose's cigarettes on the kitchen table and smoking it when everyone had gone to sleep.

This was a surreal situation, I never went out much as my parents worried so much about me. I could go to Myrtle Avenue and look at the clothes shops, truthfully now I've forgotten the names. I liked the little record shop. It sold posters too, psychedelic ones. I loved it there. That was as far as I was allowed. Oh sometimes I could go as far as Flushing, and Fairyland on Queens Boulevard, but now I was being sent to England.

I was still sitting looking out the window when I heard the alarm clock ring at 1712 Palmetto street at 6 am. I watched the train run across the rickety track. I watched Mrs. Robison walk her poodle. I watched Anna walk to Pops' for the paper. I watched my mom make tea with swollen and red eyes.

My mom bought me a new purse for the trip. Brown leather with lots of pockets. I placed the usual makeup bits, tissues, aspirin and my photos of Mom and Dad and Anthony Newley, the most important people in my now sad life.

I lay on my parents bed and they cuddled me. My father kissed me hard and gave me 500 pounds. "This will have to last you for a good while," he told me. This was a great deal of money way back then. Still is really, but then worth loads more.

And so my plane took off from JFK at 8.15. I looked back to see Mom and Dad crying. I smiled as I walked, and just a few steps later my face was sodden.

Dear Tony

I sat next to a nice lady named Bella, she told me how she was travelling to London to see her brother. She was staying in a big hotel in the West End.

A limousine was picking her up at the airport. Then it came into my head, Dad never said if I was being met. I became more frightened with each passing minute.

The plane took off. I pressed my head hard against the backrest and sobbed. Dear Bella summoned the stewardess and she said I must try to sleep. I went to the toilet and it was not me looking back from the mirror. I had hives and was swollen beyond recognition. I was given something (would never be allowed now) and I fell asleep.

I woke up in time for tea and a little sandwich and prepared to land in my new home. Bella wrote her address down for me and told me if I was ever afraid, to ring her. I never did.

I had my face pressed against the window as my plane made its descent into Heathrow. I marvelled at the beautiful lights. I knew by day England was green and lush. Tonight in the darkness, the cars resembled luminous ants.

I knew soon I would be travelling along the Great West Road (praying someone was waiting for me) to Brentford. I would look for the sign that said "Lucozade," and I would soon see the neon bottle fill the glass with the golden liquid that was so famous. I knew when I saw this that Glenhurst Road was nearby.

The plane landed at 8.50 pm. Someone helped me find my luggage and I lined up with all the people to show my passport. When I eventually walked out of Heathrow Airport, I heard a friendly voice. My cousin Pete had picked me up and I cried.

I will warn you now that those tears continued to flow fast and furious in the following days.

Great West Road, Brentford

Dear Tony

Chapter Four

I'm All I Need

June 1970s

Dear Tony,

I have not written in such a long time. You will never guess where I am — London.

Everything went wrong, but I am okay, well not really, but I will do my best.

What made me smile today? A picture of you in the *Radio Times,* like a wonderful omen to me. *Oliver Twist* was on the TV and when Grandma slept I watched it and it made me the happiest I had been in such a long time. You were a doll, you look the same to me even now.

I am going to school here and will graduate early as my parents always wanted. What I will do then, I have no idea.

I must tell you, I love Mary Quant and have spent far too much on her make-up. I guess you really didn't need to know that!

I hope one day I will see you again, you know being here, I feel closer to you. That may help me settle.

Do you like fish and chips? I'm living on them!

The East End of London is so far, but one day I hope to go and see where you were born. Do you ever miss it? Do you think about Hackney at all? I think constantly about Palmetto, perhaps too much!

Oh, I brought My pictures with me, even the one with the moustache.

Loving the music here, David Bowie, and in the local pub going to see Mott the Hoople.

Good Bye Tony,

Yes London sure swings!

Love,

Sue x

So every day was spent in school. I would come home and Nan would be home soon after. You see, respite was set up during the day as she could not be left on her own.

The long evenings were hard. I would cook the best I could on the old stove and would try to get the house right and tidy as it seemed to have been neglected for so very long. Nan would go to bed early and I would listen to the radio or watch, wait for it, *Peyton Place.*

I discovered the Harringtons at 59 Glenhurst Road!

Did I tell you the toilet was outside? Can you imagine in this day and age? The webs that covered the ceiling were covered in a thick black soot from the kerosine lamp. Every spider that lived in Brentford seemed to congregate in that old toilet. I was petrified and spent as little time as I possibly could in there.

The house was cold, not only because of the temperature, but a house devoid of love is always cold.

The only heat would come from the coal fire, and how was this girl from Brooklyn meant to light it? My aunt would light it for Nan, but I had to fend for us both now. I huffed and I puffed and still couldn't manage it. When you are freezing, you do what you have to do. Eventually with old yellow newspapers, some wood infested with little wood lice and my sheer determination, the little black orbs started to glow. My hands and my sad old heart started to warm.

Nan's cat whiskey was old, really old and dribbled. He gave up on chasing birds long ago, but would carry spiders in and then chase them, I swear I don't know how I got through those days.

Every Friday, I would drag out the tin bath that hung in the scullery and bathe in the living room. It took endless kettles to fill it, and endless pots to empty it, but eventually I looked forward to it. It was my time and I would sit there and sing my heart out.

I would sing " Cheer Up Charlie, give us a smile. What happened to that smile I use to know?" And more than anything I craved a world of "Pure Imagination." Yes, *Willy*

Wonka. I loved it and it became a new favourite. It made me so happy, and it wouldn't be too long before I had the biggest smile on my face again.

My grandma's health continued to deteriorate and she was admitted into hospital. I was really alone and although Grandma never spoke much to me, I felt so lonely and lost. There was no phone and I so wanted to speak to my mother. My aunt and uncle who were right next door were infrequent visitors.

My aunt would go out every evening to bingo, or so I thought. But later I was sure it wasn't house she was shouting!

My mother used to say to my dad, "They resented you marrying an American." Well, they certainly didn't like me very much! My two cousins had their own lives, and I must admit when we were here on holiday, they seemed to like me more. Now I never saw them. I really craved some company, someone to talk to.

I am painting a dark picture, but I am telling you the truth, I had never been so sad, so frightened, and so lonely.

School had finished and I did really well. I was proud of myself and Mom wrote how proud they were of me too. Dad was doing better and they hoped soon they could come and visit. I asked if I could come home, but someone needed to visit the hospital, and that someone would have to be for the next few weeks at least.

I guess I couldn't go home. The trunk with my things hadn't even arrived yet. I was excited about its arrival to finally see my things. I knew that would cheer me up.

I went into London sometimes just to walk around. Oh, how I loved Carnaby Street. The people looked different than they did in New York; prettier, handsomer, and the clothes. I kept thinking how my parents would react knowing I was travelling to the West End on my own. I was excited and the only thing that did make me happy was the little freedom I had. I discovered the clothing designs of BIBA, and my money was going down rapidly! I was sad and I would spend, a trait that would follow me throughout my life.

My Aunt came in one day and said I had better find a job. She said you cannot just hang around and visit the hospital. I needed a life. I was surprised at her sudden interest, even if it was to tell me off. I asked about my uncle and his health, and she said he was holding on. I craved a closeness with them, I wanted someone to tell me it would be okay.

My aunt wrote to my parents, said she was looking after me. I so wish that were true, but she never really cared about me until this job became available.

To be honest, my money was disappearing quickly, so a job would be good, especially a glamourous one. Can you imagine travelling to a foreign country and your first job is a dream one? Dancing in a beautiful club, wearing beautiful clothes. I imagined what my family and friends would say back home, Susan did good, never thought it would happen, but she did good.

My aunt knew this club in London. She worked there sometimes, and when she told them about me they were very interested. "A young American girl, very sweet natured and she loved to dance." My aunt said that is what she told them, and I better not let her down.

Raymond's
Revue Bar, 2012

Refurbished lights, 2013

Dear Tony

Chapter Five

Coldfinger

I had now a mixture of my American clothes and my BIBA clothes and I dressed up for my interview. A little extra makeup and my hair was wavy. I wore black satin trousers, A top with a sequined Charlie Chaplin on the front, and my pink and white platform shoes. I thought I looked nice. I did, I really looked nice.

I looked at the paper my aunt had written the directions on. I sure hoped Mr. Raymond would like me. Paul Raymond here I come!

It was a warm day as I stepped out of Covent Garden Station. I know it was the new Covent Garden, but since seeing *Frenzy,* the place held a kind of eerie fascination and I decided to walk to Soho. I stopped on the way and bought a few old photos in the market. One was a tea card you used to get in PG Tips, it had Anthony Newley on it, and the other pictured Michael Caine, I liked him too, from *Get Carter,* which I had recently seen.

It was a lovely warm day. I felt good. I bought an orange Jubbly and walked to Paul Raymond's.

The outside was, well to say the least, fancy. Pictures of ladies in feather boas and fancy lingerie and very little else. The lights outside were beautiful, neon and hundreds of little bulbs. Erotic dancers? I thought it said exotic, little difference really. I went in and was greeted by Janie.

"Hi, I'm Susan, I have an appointment with Mr. Raymond"

"Well, have you now? I think he will like you, Suzie." No one had ever called me Suzie, but if I got the job they could call me what they like.

I sat a minute and knew the other two girls standing in the doorway were talking about me, but I looked up and smiled and then turned away. They really were quite beautiful, and they wore false eyelashes and the thickest eyeliner. I was amazed how most girls in London resembled Dusty Springfield.

I always was quite plain, but I knew on this day I looked pretty. I felt confident.

The girls kind of parted, like the red sea did for Moses, and I knew at once that the figure approaching me was Mr Raymond.

I stood up, as my manners were always good. "Hello Sir."

He was a strange figure with a mass of hair and more gold than I had ever seen on one person. He smelt wonderful, I knew it was not Brut or Old Spice. He was not an exceptionally good looking man, but I could see how the ladies would find this gentleman attractive.

He took my hand and kissed it and said, "You are from New York, you are very young, but I like you." I smiled. "Follow me, Suzie. Let's see what we can do with you."

The walls were covered in a beautiful flocked paper, and the lights that hung from the grand ceiling must have cost a lot of money. There were bright red bulbs embedded into the ceiling and they gave off an eerie glow. The sofas were all red velvet and the air was heavy with the smell of marijuana. "Do you smoke?" he asked.

"No, Sir."

"If you want a pull, ask. It will relax you, make the interview easier."

I wanted to say, "I just had a Jubbly, but thank you all the same."

I went into a room at the top of the thick carpeted stairs, all gold and full of wall to wall mirrors. I know by now you all probably think I was stupid, but I wasn't, just naive and I so wanted a job. I wanted to dance, I wanted to be something special. I wanted to be able to shop in Biba, I wanted friends.

Mr Raymond told me to remove my top. I stood still, rigid with fear. He got close and told me to put my arms up. He slowly slid my top off and I could not move. If only my mother were here. I wanted to cry, but I kept it together.

He touched my breasts and pinched my nipples I knocked his hand away and said, "Mr. Raymond, all I wanted to do was dance, Sir."

"You will dance, but my customers expect a little more than your normal dance routine. Suzie, you are sweet and they will love you. I will teach you and the girls will help you."

I put my top on and thanked him and said I would let him know by tomorrow. He rubbed my cheek with back of his hand and then gently kissed my neck. I ran down the stairs into the air which felt good, it felt clean, The tears fell from my eyes and I watched as they hit the pavement.

"Flower in the blink of an eye, you life can change forever" — Anthony George Newley

Dear Tony

Chapter Six

After Today

August

Love Story Two

He sat across the street directly opposite Paul Raymond's outside a cafe reading the paper. There was a tea cup on the table and he was holding it tightly with his left hand.

The sun was stong and the rays of it bounced off his shiny mane of thick brown hair. A pair of sunglasses were nestled there. He wore large black rimmed glasses that seemed to dwarf his delicate face. He wore a black jumper and the collar of a blue checked shirt was visible. He wore dark denim jeans and blue canvas shoes. I never saw anyone as beautiful.

My nostrils flared and the butterflies that fluttered within me must have been wearing Doc Martins. Have you ever felt you are going to be sick and you flare your nostrils and do whatever you can to keep the contents of your stomach where they should be?

I was out of breath and for one minute I thought everyone could hear the beating of my heart. I stood there sniffing. I had to do this, I had to go over. I went to walk then stopped, went forward again my legs wouldn't move.

I could not let this moment pass, I had to after all these years, how could I chicken out now?

I stepped out and heard the car beep as I nearly got hit, he looked up and was the handsomest man I had ever seen. Yes older than when I first saw him, but truly perfect.

"Hello Mr. Newley."

He looked up and smiled that smile.

"May I please have an autograph?" I handed him the little tea card and he smiled.

"They haven't invented a pen small enough to sign this," he laughed.

He ran his finger over my cheek and then looked, his finger was covered in my best Mary Quant. I had forgotten to check my face.

"Sit down, Flower, you need more than an autograph, have a coffee?"

"Oh yes, please," I said, in a desperate voice I regret to this day! I wanted to say, "It's me, Susan Newman, do you remember me?"

I could hardly speak, but then our words started to come easy. I think on this bright sunny day, in Soho, two lonely souls found each other.

Tony spoke of his children and the gap he felt in his life since his marriage had broken up. I remember reading about it in the paper and confess to smiling at the time, but now I felt so sad for him, for the second time in my life I wanted to hug him. He took pictures out of his wallet, his dear children in all different poses and places. The park, the garden, in his arms.

"I am so very sorry," I said. "Your children are very beautiful."

"Yes, they are." he said with his head hung low. "I still see them all the time." I patted his hand, the one that held the pictures and he smiled.

It seemed funny that my idol, my prince, was sitting here telling me his sad stories. I felt as if I was sitting with an old friend (in many ways I was), should you be telling me these things Tony? Don't stop! I told him why I had been crying and he was upset, really upset.

"Well we can tell them tomorrow you definitely won't be taking that job. I know Paul and it will be fine. Why did you go there?"

"I need to work."

"You will one day, but not in there." He stroked my cheek again. Did he say tomorrow? Would there be a tomorrow?

I told him about New York and my little story, I wanted to say, "But hey, you know that as I having been writing to you for years." I mentioned the pictures he had sent me.

"I can't say I read every letter. Most of them I do, but I have a lovely girl who helps me out."

I kept thinking of the words I wrote in those letters. Was I stupid to think he actually had read them? But still that thought kept me going on many a day. So, Mr Newley, you might never have even known me if it hadn't been for today. Somehow at that very moment what had gone on only an hour or so before didn't seem so bad!

Dear Tony

We had another drink. This time I had tea and we shared a big biscuit. It was tired up in pretty gold ribbon (I still have it). Tony spoke of *Doctor Doolittle* (after I mentioned my "Mugg" shot). He made me laugh with all his stories and of Mr. Harrison, "God's gift to no one," he called him. "Oh, he hated me, Flower. I could do nothing right. Bricusse put himself out there for me (he asked if I knew who Leslie Bricusse was), "But in the end I got me own back. But that is for a different time", he smiled. I can't disclose what Tony told me, but you would all be jolly proud!

"The animals loved me, but why not? Look at me," and we laughed.

"I'm glad you are smiling again, it suits you," he said.

He asked me if I had seen *Sammy Lee,* a film he had made in the 60s in the same street we were having our tea, which I had not. "You will see it with me," he said. I wondered how much my heart could take today.

Tony got up and paid for the tea. I was surprised to see how small and fragile he appeared. When I had seen him on the stage, he looked huge to my 9 year old eyes. We walked and we talked, and we laughed and I hadn't been this happy for such a long time. I told him my story of seeing him on Broadway, and how *Roar* had changed my life. I said how I cried when he fell to his knees and sang. He gently took my face in his hands and said "I remember you, Flower." I cried again.

We walked all around Soho. It was full of wonderful characters and the best sex shops I had ever seen, probably the only sex shops I had ever seen. Neon lights shone everywhere, and this Soho really was quite beautiful. Tony held my hand as we walked, and Soho took on this amazing neon glow. I glowed, too.

"Do you like Chinese?"

"Yes, very much, I replied. My response was so quick. Let me be honest. Even If I known I was going to get hives again, if I would have ended up looking like an oompa loompa by the end of the night, I would still have said yes. The thought even after such a short time of saying "Goodbye, Mr. Newley" filled me with sadness.

We ate in a restaurant that was featured in *Sammy Lee.* I can't remember the food, or the decor, but I do remember that the day we met was the best day of my life.

Even today I still take my trip to Soho. Raymond's is just a shell and our cafe a smoothie shop, but I still go, and toast him every year on our anniversary.

As the night progressed our friendship was well underway, and it would remain solid throughout the many years that followed.

Tony would confide in me and I would always say what I thought Tony needed to hear. I might have really wanted to say something strong or have a real go at him, but I decided at that very moment that I would do whatever I could to keep him in my life. So began the roller coaster of the Newman/Newley friendship.

I knew the name of each girl he met. I even became friends with his "Tink." I never was going to be the one to tell him off, or show my disappointment. He had enough of that from other people. I would be the one he trusted with his deepest, darkest secrets. I would be the one who stayed in the background and would come out when he needed me. Tony always said I was the constant light in his darkness, and he was my calm after the most beautiful storm. When you have something so precious in your grasp you do anything to keep it there. I worked hard to keep it there.

So after our meal and our getting to know you conversation these words followed and my life would change forever.

"I will get my driver to take us home."

I loved him since I was 9, you know that kind of crush love you have for everyone on the telly, or the handsome school teacher or for Pee Wee Pollock. Did you ever put someone you don't know on the highest pedestal and you finally get to met them and it topples over? This pedestal I put Mr. Newley on was not high enough! So on a warm night in Soho, London, I fell in love for real.

Dear Tony,

How can I sleep? I fear if I close my eyes I will wake and this will be a dream. Instead I would rather lie here and just watch you breathe.

I can touch you, feel your beautiful face and smell your hair.

There will be time for sleep, tonight is not one of them.

I love you Tony,

I think I always have, I think I always will.

Sue xx

Chapter Seven

Feeling Good

Our days were spent talking and Tony would write. I would listen to music, and make cups of tea, endless cups of tea. He would stop from time to time and tell me a story. Sometimes I could not stop laughing, sometimes I cried.

I was young, and still I knew that this incredible man that sat before me was so unhappy and insecure I didn't understand it fully at the time, but as our years together rolled on, I understood him more .

You left the things you loved most, just in case they left you first. I will never leave you!

We did what we could to Glenhurst Road to make it comfortable, somehow to make it ours. In the long kitchen Tony set up a makeshift shower. Oh, the luxury.

How could he want to stay here? I was afraid to ask the question.

He took me to Oswald Street to see where he grew up. It looked sad and the houses would soon be demolished. I was fascinated by his stories of childhood, but that is for another story that will be told, all in good time. Enough material there for another volume.

On most days we would walk to the park and look at the flowers and trees and just the simplest of life's pleasure became an adventure with him.

Anthony, you know in the beginning I could not call him Tony, was special and I wanted him to know. I didn't want to be…I can't finish this sentence as I wasn't sure how I should be with him. He was as childlike at times as I was. Sometimes I forgot just how old he was, which was a good thing. And at other times I was the adult, and he would listen and respond to me.

Tony was not like a "star." Oh, he shone bright alright, but he was just a nice man, caring, considerate, loving and gracious and totally insecure. He constantly questioned his work, his ability, his looks. He was not at all like the man I had watched and admired. I believed in him after my first milky coffee, now could I get him to believe in himself?

Now as an adult who experienced the "The Magic of Newley" and seven years training as a therapist, I know this dear man was depressed and had issues it would take years for him to finally understand and that makes me so very sad. It makes me sad to think that just when he was starting to become more comfortable with himself he left us.

Tony had a phone installed, as phones were still quite rare in households. He needed to be able to be contacted and I for the first time I could call home. I didn't begin to know how to thank him. I mean this beautiful man, this man I loved, was here in my house with the dribbling cat, the makeshift shower and the outside loo and we were happy. He was happy.

On the days he would go to see the children, I was prepared for his return. He would be quiet and withdrawn. I would make something simple to eat (thank goodness his palate was plain). Cheese on toast was the best I could do at that time. I would talk to him quietly and encourage him to write or go for a walk, but at least to talk to me.

Dear Tony,

Did I even exist before I met you? Will I be able to survive if the day comes when I look and you are no longer here?

How can you be you, my darling, and not be happy. I want to quote all your lyrics, but knew this will drive you mad.

 "Look at your face just look at it."

"Where would I be without you Tony?"

"My first love. No one ever needed my love before."

But instead I took the journey at your pace and the days and years that follow will make me think I did the right thing.

So if you wake up happy, I smile. If you cry by lunch time, I will hold you. If you laugh at teatime, I will join in with your silly jokes. If you withdraw by the evening, I will tuck you in so tight and whisper in your ear it will be okay.

You see Tony when someone loves you as much as I do, it will always be okay.

I love you. Mr. Newley,

Sue xx

There were times over the many years I wanted to cry. When he told me about the other girls, I wanted to tell him I had enough. I wanted to ask him why, why he tried to sabotage every good thing in his life. I never asked.

I kept a diary when I met Tony. I never wanted to forget the joy I experienced or to coin my phrase "The magic of Newley." This is the first time I have really shared my story with anyone. I hope you all know how privileged you are!

I celebrated Tony's birthday with him and it was a milestone one to boot! What do you buy someone like Tony? He asked for new underwear. Well yes, of course. What else to you expect to buy for your British superstar love? I bought him his pants (red ones!) and socks, he loved his socks! I also bought a beautiful pen with a gold musical note on it. I have it now. Maybe I can sign a book with it, someday!

Tony was sad the morning of his birthday and I knew more than anything he wanted to be with his family. He did manage to spend some precious time with the children that afternoon and that cheered him up for the rest of the day.

I sang Happy Birthday in my shrill American drawl. Tony sang " Who Can I Turn To?" to me. That evening we had a simple dinner, and a cake I had made with pretty blue frosting adorned with a heart and multi-coloured candles. We had each other. I wish I would have blown out those candles, I know what my wish would have been!

Dear Tony,

Just think of all the birthdays we can celebrate together!

Maybe next year we can go to a fancy restaurant. I will dress up and walk in on your arm and people will look up and gasp.

Tonight I will dream about you and all the days ahead. I am glad you had a nice birthday.

I love you, Tony,

Sue xx

Dear Tony

Chapter Eight

Falling in Love Again

Saturday

I woke up early and watched Tony compose. I can't explain what watching a genius looks like. It was all facial expressions and those eyebrows had a life of their own. His hands would move effortlessly as if an orchestra was watching his every move. He kept his eyes tightly closed and each note high and low was captured in those hands. Sometimes he would write something down, not music, but a guide word he would understand. Music and words were created together in that beautiful head.

Sometimes it took much prompting to get Tony started, but once he began he was disciplined and would carry on until he felt he had finished.

Then after a quick glimpse nothing was mentioned. I did not speak during this process, but merely became an observer of his world and how honoured I was.

His description of "Today, Tomorrow, and Yesterday:" "I can hear it, every instrument, every dip, every high. I can hear the singers."

I could hear it too as he demonstrated what would be the music for *The Good Old Bad Old Days*. I loved the score even before I knew exactly what the show would be about. I knew in the very near future he was going to meet with Bricusse, but I did not let myself think when this was to be.

On this Saturday we went shopping, tonight we were going out. A proper, special night out. Tony's friend Sammy Davis Jr. (OMG) was doing a few impromptu numbers in a club in London and we had to go.

Tony bought me a black dress, my very first little black dress. It was covered around the neckline with gold sequins that hung in shapes like little castinets. It was beautiful. I wore black and gold stilettos and towered above my handsome companion, and yet he was bigger than anyone I had ever met.

I felt beautiful for the first time! Even Tony told me I was beautiful, and when you are told by someone like Anthony Newley you want to believe it to be true.

So with more lacquer in my hair than remained in the tin, and eyeliner Dusty would be proud of we left.

Tony's driver picked us up and into the West End we went to The Bag Of Nails, the club in Soho, and it was like something I saw on an old TV show.

I felt odd the minute I walked through the door. I didn't belong here, not amongst these beautiful people. Truly this was a scary place for me. Everyone, and I mean everyone, was elegant and dressed so beautifully. Sitting in the car I felt so pretty and grown up; sitting in the Bag Of Nails I felt non-existent.

We sat having a drink, I had dry martini with ice and a slice, Tony had a large white wine. My eyes went from the statuesque redhead at the bar to the petite blonde who sat opposite us, and the two of them and every other woman in the club was staring at Tony. I think the men were too. One of the waiters was talking and I saw Tony jump up, I think he said something about me. Tony gently took him by the elbow and had a word. I was embarrassed. Why was he with me?

I was introduced to Sammy Davis, I extended my hand and smiled. Sammy was nice and I bent down and he gave me a kiss on both cheeks, part of me expected him to take Tony by the shoulders and say "Why, Newberg?" But he was kind.

What did amaze me was how small Sammy really was, smaller than my Tony. Yet these two together were the biggest presence in the whole place!

They were like two schoolboys, hugging one minute and giving those little punches you give to someone you care for. It was obvious even to the untrained eye that these two loved one another. They were discussing an upcoming project they were working on. I could only imagine in my mind how wonderful it would be seeing them work together. I heard Tony mention a few songs, Sammy smoking and drinking whiskey nodded constantly like one of those dogs you place in the back of your car. Raucous laughter echoed off the walls. Yes, these two wonderful men were quite an amazing sight to behold! I wondered what they were planning and I knew Tony would tell me .

The *Burt Bacharach Special* was in the planning stages, and we all know how that turned out!

Out of the corner of my eye I saw a face that I recognised, David Hemmings was there with his wife Gayle Hunnicut. Tony hugged them both, I don't know who was prettier, David or Gayle. I went red and sat down.

Sammy sang "Fool", and dedicated it to Tony, the crowd went wild, followed swiftly by his signature tune, "The Candy Man," and finished with the Bricusse song from *Doolittle*,

Dear Tony

When I Look In Your Eyes." Tony tapped me and smiled and made the sign of an X with his fingers, his way of swearing at REX so nobody knew. He was so funny. He told me his story of working with Mr. Harrison, he said, "You know, Flower, that seal went to the North Pole after the shoot in the hope the cold would somehow numb her brain and she could forget working with that pompous ass!"

The crowd were calling for Tony to sing. Tony stood and bowed, he blew kisses. Sammy ran to the door and kissed him. They hugged. Sammy kissed my hand and we left.

A wonderful night, but I felt awkward. Someone like Tony deserved to have the best of everything. I was a love-struck young woman, and I could not have been further from his beautiful ex-wife if I had tried. I did love him though, this is one thing I was sure of. He never said, but I knew he cared for me. In the car I put my head on his shoulder and said, "Tony, I'm sorry." He sat bolt upright, "Flower, don't you ever apologize for being yourself," That was all he said, that was enough.

Dear Tony,

I heard you on the phone. I know our time together is coming to an end. I also know you don't want to tell me.

I heard you singing to Bricusse on the phone "Today," "Tomorrow,",and "Yesterday." Had I heard them completed before anyone else? Was Bricusse the second person you sang them to?

How long would I have to wait for you to sing to "Who Can I Turn To?"again? I will miss your answer, "Surely love, you are sick of that song?"

How will I wake up when you are not here? You can't go yet. You "Promised Me a Love Song."

I won't ever say goodbye,

Sue x

Tuesday

I could not get Tony to get up today. He was very low, the children were away with their mum and I guessed this was the reason.

Tony was writing, he was going to star in a new film based on *The Old Curiosity Shop*.

"Get up, Tony. Come on, you promised you would write. I made a nice breakfast and then we can have a walk. Come on love, please."

"You remind me at times of Sara Deever, another New Yorker who could be a real pain in the ass."

Any time after this when I would push him or tell him off he called me Sara. Oh, if only I would have been Sara, Charlie would have never walked out that door! Just in case some of you don't know, Sara Deever was a character in *Sweet November,* the most beautiful love story.

Tony ate his eggs, showered and we went to Boston Manor park.

Tony would speak to the flowers as if they were little fairies in disguise. "Look at them, works of art with a heart," he would meditate and this would energise him. Tony was very spiritual and most things fascinated him. I know he could be jolly hard work, but the boy within him was still full of joy and wonder. I so hoped he would never lose that, as that is what made Newley, Newley!

As we approached the alley that ran behind 59, we stopped to speak with Mr Smith. He was a lovely old boy who sat day after day making stools, weaving them intricately by hand. His hands, rough and dirty, were extended to Tony who returned the gesture willingly. Not many people liked "Smithy" as he could be brash, but he loved me. When I used to visit as a child I would sit for hours with him and was fascinated by what he did.

I thought he may have asked who Tony was, but he kept on with his weaving as we walked away. Just as we were about to turn the corner he shouted, "Stop The World!" Tony looked back and waved.

When we got home Tony exercised (which he did on a daily basis), wrote, and just when I thought he couldn't write anything better, he did.

He was composing the music for *Quilp.* "I've forgotten how we met, but did I live one hour before?" from "Love Has the Longest Memory of All." He was a story telling genius. I loved those lyrics so very much.

That night we walked up the Great West road and bought fish and chips. The old man who owned the chippie was lovely and had a curved spine. Tony would always make him laugh, and years later he told me his Daniel Quilp was based on the Brentford chippie.

Dear Tony

Chapter Nine

Laugh

Dear Tony,

Thank you for the beautiful masterpiece that you drew for me. I will cherish it and when we are old and gray, it will hang above the finest marble fireplace in our home. When guests come for dinner they will admire it.

I will stand there in my velvet gown and say, "That's My Boy!" You will always be my boy.

I love you,

Sue xx

I want to include some lighthearted moments. There were so many. When Tony was on form there was no one like him. Here are two that are so very precious to me.

One day I came out of the shower to see a little picture drawn on my lined note pad that always sat on the dining room table.

"What is that, Tony?"

"Look closely darling," Tony replied.

"Is it a rocket?"

Tony laughed hysterically. "No, Flower, it's me, I did you a portrait of my love."

"Oh, my God, Tony, it is beautiful. But it still looks like a rocket."

Then Tony began countdown, "Ten, Nine, Eight…"

"Stop right there, mister." We both continued to laugh.

On another occasion, woke up and went downstairs to hear water running. I knew Tony must have been in the shower. I opened the back door and waved to my next door neighbour, who was pegging out the wash.

Debbie and Donna were a lovely couple, both ambulance drivers. They had been so helpful and kind to me when Nan first got sick. Debbie signaled for me to come to the fence.

"Can I ask you a question? Have you got Anthony Newley staying with you?"

"Shhhh," I said. "He's my dad's cousin, and he is going through a rough time, He is staying here to rest."

I saw Debbie's expression change and I followed her eyes and turned. There was Tony, stark naked, smoking a joint. He nodded and smiled and walked back inside.

"What a close family you are," Debbie said. She winked and went into her house.

He was the kindest, funniest man. He had the greatest, wicked sense of humour, I loved it when he was like this, like a boy. He was playful like your favorite puppy.

Whether in his 30s, 40s, 50s, or 60s, I knew in my heart he would always be my beautiful boy!

And that little picture I mentioned above, do I still have it? Yes, of course I do. It is sealed in plastic and is in a little white envelope marked: NEWLEY A Very Rare Specimen.

Chapter Ten

Lunch with a Friend

Thursday, November

I was in for a beautiful surprise, Tony was taking me to Southend, the seaside. We were both like kids.

We took a thermos of tea. This man and his tea could never be parted!

Tony's driver picked us up at the start of a beautiful, surreal, magical day. There was a slight nip in the air, but the sun shone bright.

I wish you could have seen his face as we approached Southend. You could hear the funfair music and he squeezed my hand in excitement. We could see the Big wheel in the Kursaal. This was a proper amusement park, with hundreds of lights flickering, children screaming as they soared into the air, and everyone's granddad walking around with a hankie tied to his head to keep off the sun. The hats that sat on heads were emblazoned with "Kiss Me Quick."

"What should we do first, darling?" I wanted to say sit and watch, but I knew I was in for a ride on something. The Waltzer it was then.

For my American friends, this is a bit like a whip on cocaine. You are flung around by men who take their lives in their hands. As the ride moves, they jump on and spin your car manually! Tony screeched in delight and I just screeched. I held him so tight, and one point when I managed to lift my broken neck, I saw the biggest smile on his face. It made me so happy.

Tony's delicate stomach had a workout this day with hot dogs (yes, more than one). We shared candy floss and kissed the sugar off each others' lips, and we had warm doughnuts covered in cinnamon.

We walked along the pier and played penny arcade games. My favourite was these little scenes that you put money in, and watch as scenes come alive. One was a woman laying in bed and a ghost comes and everything shook. It was fascinating.

What was more fascinating was seeing my darling friend being so happy. Tony was stopped a few times and he gave autographs graciously. He was full of joy that day.

On the seafront we joined in with the other "kids" and watched Punch and Judy. That's The Way To Do It, oh yes it most certainly was!

We ran to the water. He rolled up his trousers and we both waded in the freezing sea, and it really was freezing. Then we lay on the sand, close to each other to keep warm. We stayed there for ages not talking, but just looking at the sky.

We walked back to the Kursal and looked at all the clown heads that were sculpted on the awnings, so beautiful and painted to perfection. Tony traced every line in their crooked faces with his finger.

We had tea (seaside tea tastes the best), and shared a bag of chips and Tony called for the car to take us home.

We sat in the back of the car quietly at first, trying to make sense of the magic that had gone on. Tony told me he loved me. I nodded, as my mouth would not work, and squeezed his hand and he laid his head on my lap and smiled. He had my response and I never had to utter a word.

What would I do without you Tony, please tell me what shall I do?

I was about to find out.

Southend Rock (candy)

Dear Tony

Chapter Eleven

I Do Not Love You

The following day the sun never came out and the sky was so gray, apt really!

Tony went to see his children. I did a little shopping. I was surprised when he returned and suggested we go out again that night. We went to Richmond to have dinner.

It was cold as we stood by the river. The lights from the buildings reflected off the water. The water that fell from my eyes burnt my cold cheeks.

Tony told me he was going to Los Angeles in the morning. I held on to him so tight, we stayed that way for what seemed like hours. I was afraid to let go, I was so afraid! I sobbed into his shoulder and then looked straight into his eyes and said, "I love you Tony, I love you so much"

"Do you really, Flower? Do you? Darling, you don't really know what love is."

My voice raised and cracking, I said, "I can't think of a time when I haven't loved you Tony, please don't treat me like a child! We have been together months. I know what love is, I know only too well! I had the best teacher!"

We both cried, and went "home" for the last time. When we got back I made tea, Tony sat at the table and wrote. Tony had written a poem for me. I constantly asked for him to write something for me. I was so sad and he was too. He wrote me a poem and threw it away and said one day he would write something worthy of me. I retrieved my poem from the bin and till this day cherish it.

Two of Mr. Newley's finest compositions are my songs, and I listen to them both on a daily basis. The poem now set to music is one of them.

That morning after tea and tears I walked down the passage way with the love of my life. I never said "Goodbye, Tony," I just very gently closed the door to number 59.

I stood with my head against the door as if I was glued there. When I managed to move, I ran to the window just as the car was driving away. I saw Tony look back through the rear car window, I collapsed and remained on my knees sobbing until I was numb.

I didn't think I could go on. I went into the dining room and lit the fire, hoping that sitting and watching the flames would somehow warm me. I felt like a block of ice, I felt like someone had taken my soul. There was somewhere else I needed to go.

I remember the journey I took up the stairs, into what was our room. The bed was not made, but was rumpled, I launched on it as if I was a great Olympian preparing for a dive. I wailed like an injured animal. I laid on his pillow, the aroma of Olbas oil and lavender filled my nostrils and I slept until the sound of the phone woke me.

I charged down the steep stairs and grabbed the phone on its third ring. It was my mom, not who I had hoped, but the voice brought me comfort all the same.

Dear Tony,

I spend my days at the hospital, Nan is doing better, but remains confused.

I wanted to thank you for your offer to send me to The Royal Academy of Dramatic Arts, but my heart is out of sync at the moment, and I have not said that to make you feel bad.

I found a few of your things, maybe one day you'll come pick them up. Do you think you will?

Oh I miss you so very much. Please call me again, I won't cry, I promise! I wear the ring and never ever take it off.

I spoke to my parents and my mom might try to come for Christmas. I am dreading Christmas. I hope you get to see the children, I know that will bring you such joy.

I have applied for a little job, and I hope I get it as it will keep me busy.

I hope all is going good with the show. I can't wait until you are here again.

I know you will be so busy, but just one dinner will make me so happy.

Take care Tone,

I love you,

Sue x

Chapter Twelve

I'll Begin Again

December

My mother did come for Christmas and I told her about my friendship with Tony. Of course, a mother wants only good for her children. I know that now. When my mother could see how much I cared for Tony, she listened to my stories and seemed to accept the situation. I think Mom did this as we had missed each other so very much and to have been angry would have been a waste.

My mom spoke to Tony a few times on the phone and said he does sound like a lovely man. She always had great taste, my mom. She would always stumble with her words when talking to him. "Oh dear, that was Anthony Newley I just spoke to!"

We spent a lovely two weeks together. We shopped, went to the odd castle, but mainly we got to know each other all over again! We visited Nan who was becoming more and more confused. "Soon you'll be able to come home," Mom said, but I couldn't. What if Tony came back? He would need me, wouldn't he?

My mother's visit ended far too soon.

Dear Tony,

My mum left today, I hate all these goodbyes.

I hope you are well, my darling, and perhaps missing me as much as I am missing you! I crave to feel you in my arms, but you are so very busy. I know that if you could be here with me you would.

I 'll wait patiently.

Be happy my darling friend.

I love you,

Sue xxx

January

The phone call

Oh, Tony. It is so good to hear your voice. How are you, and how is the family? I can't wait till next month to see you, It seems so long. No, sorry love, you talk. You have! Where did you meet? Yes, she sounds lovely, Tony. Of course I only ever wanted you to be happy. Yes, I know if things were different. Surprised? Maybe a little and a bit disappoint…no, Darling, it doesn't matter.

I'm okay, yes all going good, no, you go and we'll talk soon. Yes send me some pictures I would love that.

No, I'm okay, really.

Be happy, yes I love you too.

Goodbye, Tony

I took to my bed for a week, I lost my job, I lost my reason for living.

I never said "How could you?" or "You knew how much I loved you," or "I decided to stay here because of you," I just said, "I want you to be happy, Tony, and in my heart that is all I really did want, but how can I accept you are now with someone else? How?"

February

It was very cold, and the house seemed even colder now. I made a friend called Val and sometimes we went to the pub for a drink. We went to the movies and saw some great scary films, and I discovered Oliver Reed.

The morning of my birthday, I ran down the stairs and hoped one of my two cards would be from Tony. Mom and Dad sent a beautiful one and put $50.00 in it. They also wrote they would call me on my birthday, so I had so much to look forward to. I had one from my dear Aunt Rose with money in it too.

Nothing from Tony. Maybe he will call or contact me when the show opens.

I went shopping, changed my money into Sterling and bought a new blouse. I also intended to treat myself to Chinese food.

At about 7 o'clock, there was a knock at the door. I opened the door to be confronted with a bunch of shiny red balloons made of foil. I had not seen ones like that before. The beautiful person holding the balloons made me cry.

"Flower, I would never forget your birthday"

Tony was here for the show rehearsals, he was with his new lady, but he did this for me. All the years that followed, Tony always remembered my birthday.

We went out for dinner and when we came home he wanted me to pop the balloons. This upset me so much, because they were beautiful. "I'll buy you more," he said, "Please pop the balloons."

I took a pin and popped the balloons. Popping the fourth one, something fell to the floor. There was a beautiful ring, one he had worn and I admired. To this day I have never taken that ring off. I have a piece of my Tony wherever I go.

That night ended far too quickly, but it would be a birthday I would never forget.

The tea card

Bubba, our little devil, from THE GOOD OLD BAD OLD DAYS

Dear Tony

Chapter Thirteen

Here I'll Stay

So I lived my life to the best of my ability and waited patiently for Tony's return to England and the West End.

The Good Old Bad Old Days opened and I took my place in the audience amongst all the other eager Newley lovers. Tony looked wonderful and his big bouncy devil tail and horns suited him, perhaps too well! The sets and the colours were beautiful and how extraordinarily different from *Roar of the Greasepaint*.

This show was big in every sense of the word. There was so much going on you were not sure what to look at first. It was loud and absolutely wonderful! *The GOBODS* was stunning and a show that should have found its way to Broadway. It did not!

I sat there and listened to the songs Tony had played a part in writing. My only regret was that "I Do Not Love You" was not performed by him, as he sang it many times to me and it made my heart melt.

This was a grand show, this was a Newley showcase, so why were people leaving before it had finished? Again Leslie and Tony were ground breaking, but the public were not ready. I wondered if they ever would be.

Dear Tony,

I love the show and your lady is very beautiful.

You, as always, are wonderful and the music I saw you create is amazing.

I'm sorry about the reviews, as you always said, "What is it they really want from me?" In fact, they love you, It's the show they are not keen on! "Forgettable music," they said, I will never forget it, I love it.

When I was at the matinée some people got up and left, I was angry for you. I followed them and said they wouldn't know a good show if it bit them on the ass!

I hope things get better for you and you will now always be happy, my darling friend.

I hope we can talk soon, or have a drink, even a spot of tea will do!

Goodbye Tony

I love you,

Sue x

A Phone call

Tony,

How wonderful to hear from you. How is the show going now? Oh, I am so very sorry. I have seen it ten times. Yes, I saw you smile at me the other day.

When? Congratulations! You're a great dad, I know how much your children mean to you. Yes, you must keep in touch.

I hope you start to feel better soon. Maybe now you can rest. You're not getting any younger, Mr. Newley. You looked tired, please look after yourself

Do you think you'll ever come back to visit?

Yes, that is a great deal of money and it is something you are so wonderful at, and one day I will come and see you in Vegas, I promise.

Yes darling, I'll be here always waiting for you,

You too, of course I love you

Goodbye Tony

So my dear man was now really happy and I again went away and cried.

I only found out Tony was real sick because I read it in the paper.

The Good Old Bad Old Days closed and he was not well when he returned home. I could not write as I knew he would not be able to pick up his mail. I rang his service and one of the lovely ladies who knew me well said he had become very run down and it was taking longer than normal to recuperate, but she would tell him I called.

So I waited and prayed that dear Tony would soon be well. I waited so long to hear about him.

I read an interview that said Tony was headed for Vegas, and that Leslie Bricusse was upset they would not be working together again for quite a while. I was sad too.

It had been months and…

A Phone call

"Hello, Flower."

I was so happy to hear his voice.

Tony,

How are you? I was so worried. Why didn't you write?

Congratulations! A little girl, beautiful name, and I know you will all be very happy. A new relationship and a new baby, and your parents. That is an amazing story, it just seems everything is going so well for you. Of course I'm happy, if you are.

Don't say that, Darling, get to know him better. I know he was different than what you imagined. But he is your dad and that is something you always wanted, Darling.

Tony, my Nan died. Yes, it is very sad. No, Darling, I'm okay. Yes, working hard. Life is good as you say.

I hope someday soon we can share that tea, sod the tea, champagne it will be.

I will, I'll write soon, be happy always, my darling friend,

I love you too,

Goodbye Tony

Anthony Newley stops the world once again with songs and laughter... it's something to shout about, and fall in love with too!

Mr. Quilp

Musical Adaptation of Charles Dickens' 'The Old Curiosity Shop'

a Reader's Digest film...

Anthony Newley *starring as* 'Mr. Quilp' *also starring* David Hemmings

David Warner · Michael Hordern · Paul Rogers · Jill Bennett · Mona Washbourne · Peter Duncan
and introducing Sarah Jane Varley *as* Nell · Sarah Webb *as* Duchess · *Directed by* Michael Tuchner · *Music and Lyrics by* Anthony Newley
Music supervised and conducted by Elmer Bernstein · *Screenplay by* Louis *and* Irene Kamp · *Musical Numbers staged by* Gillian Lynne
Produced by Helen M. Strauss · in color ▲E Avco Embassy Pictures Release G GENERAL AUDIENCES

Dear Tony

Chapter Fourteen

Somewhere

Dear Tony,

Quilp will be wonderful, as that is all you can ever be!

I told Jack the chippie what you said about him being like Daniel Quilp, and oh, he did laugh. Every time I eat chips I think of you, I think of us.

I can't wait to see it. I hope your family and you have a wonderful time here. I saw the baby and you both in the paper. You are all so beautiful!

I will be thinking of you. Break a leg, darling friend.

I love you,

Sue xx

Tony came back to England to film *Mr Quilp*.

He had brought his family and he seemed very happy. I read countless interviews in the paper and saw him interviewed on the BBC.

I received a phone call by one of Tony's assistants to see if I could meet him for lunch. Tony's wife and daughter were extras in *Quilp*, so I was surprised we were able to meet. We had that tea and Tony was filled with ideas of what he was going to do. A new album, "A special one," he said. "There is a new show I'm working on. I have wanted to do it for years."

I knew he meant *Chaplin* as he spoke about it so many times. He was not so fascinated with Chaplin's work as he was with Chaplin the man, and I knew if anyone could do it, Newley could.

He had so many projects on the go to raise funds for the show.

You all know about *The Garbage Pail* kids, and *It Seemed A Good Idea At the Time*, Las Vegas was ongoing and so were his dreams. Tony seemed happy and relaxed or as happy and relaxed as he could ever be.

We kept in contact by phone and letter as often as we could.

American TV kept him pretty busy with endless appearances on quiz shows (which he absolutely hated), the odd TV series, and chat shows galore. Tony sent some pictures to me he had done while recording his new album. He looked wonderful, relaxed, and happy and I so hoped this would always be the case.

Chapter Fifteen

On a Wonderful Day Like Today

Dear Tony,

Yes, married life will be good. He is a wonderful man. I got my Englishman after all, and I am very lucky. I guess England will always be home now, somehow I can't leave. I wonder if you know the real reason why?

Think of me on my day, I will try not to think of you!

I love you,

Sue xxx

I married in 1975 to a wonderful man who knew I had been in love before, just as he himself had, but no questions were asked, and no information was volunteered. I knew I was lucky to find love again. Tony sent us a wedding present and we bought the contents of my new home with his generous gift.

I was so aware, especially in later years, that I stayed here originally for Newley and yet he settled in America and made all these shows I would never get to see until much later.

I did see Tony briefly in London when he came to London on business. He was again working with Leslie Bricusse on a new version of *Peter Pan* for American TV. The score was magic as always and I was so looking forward to seeing this version.

I am aware there are many gaps in Tony's career here, but it is more about Newley the man than the star I am trying to show you.

1982

While we are talking about wonderful men, I lost my father after years of suffering. My parents at this time had moved to Florida, as the warmth gave my dad comfort.

I called Tony's answering service to let him know and he attended the funeral and took me, my mum and the girls to dinner afterwards. My youngest daughter was fascinated with Tony's face and his eyebrows, and as she sat in her highchair she constantly touched him. It wasn't until we left the restaurant that we saw the spaghetti hanging from his brow. He was and always will be one of the dearest friends I would ever have.

Tony was in London again looking into doing a show with Bruce Forsyth featuring all the music written by Newley/Bricusse. Tony was very excited to be working with Bruce again, reprising the role he had played in *Heironymus Merkin.*

The show, like *Peter Pan,* was not the great success we were all hoping for, and once again I saw the frustrated, sad Newley emerge. "It seems I can do no right," he would say time and time again.

Tony had won The Entertainer of the Year award in Las Vegas three times, but in his mind this was never where he wanted to be. This was not being creative, this was standing on a stage singing the same songs over and over again, cracking the same jokes everyone has heard a dozen times before, and smiling when inside he was falling apart. It was bringing in mega money yet he was so unhappy.

He had been told by some people to not complain and just "do what you are good at" and keep singing. Of course they could see pound and dollar signs, but I saw the tears!

"Do what your good at?" What wasn't he good at, and there lies the problem.

You have this gentle, misguided genius who at times didn't know where to turn. I would be rich if I had a pound for every time he asked me what should I do? "Follow your heart and dreams, Tony," just as you tell everyone else to do.

Tony had become a dad again, but still he lacked the joy I had once observed.

It would take a few years, but Tony did follow his heart. I first heard about this idea in the early seventies, and now it was actually going to happen. Tony was animated and excited, that made me so excited too.

Chaplin, produced in 1983, a collaboration with Stanley Ralph Ross did not go as well as planned. At one point Tony had said he wished he could done it on his own. I too wished he had. Stanley Ralph Ross was difficult and in my honest opinion, Tony deserved

Dear Tony

better, far better. I did not like him and I felt he took advantage of Tony's kindness and generosity. Tony had songs cut, great songs and was not in control of this show.

The 1985 version was far better, Tony's songs were reintroduced and he directed, but just as his dream of appearing on Broadway again was about to happen, the backers pulled out.

In Las Vegas

Tony and Sammy Davis Jr. from the 1972 Burt Bacharach TV special,
from Tony's private collection

Dear Tony

Chapter Sixteen

Old Bones

Dear Tony,

Where do I begin? I am so sorry. I knew you wanted this show to be a success more than anything, No, I disagree. There are many more wonderful things you will do. I know that head is jam packed with magic!

I hope you will get good results from the hospital, and I am so angry you left it so long. I told you a long time ago you weren't right, but as usual you never listen. You start looking after yourself, you are so loved.

I hope your family are all well. We are all fine. Please let me know as soon as you can how you are.

You, Mr. Newley, could never be a failure in my eyes or anyone else's. Only you think that, Tony, and you must stop. A "Little Chap" you may be, but you will always be a giant to me.

I love you,

Goodbye Tony,

Sue x

Tony had an exploratory operation and was diagnosed with renal cancer in 1985. The operation to remove the cancerous kidney went really well and it was not long before Tony was working again. One favourite...

He played the wonderful Mad Hatter in *Alice in Wonderland* produced for CBS in the United States. I have spoken to a few people involved with this project since Tony has died and they have all told me there would have been no production without Tony Newley. The director was a disaster and Tony took everyone under his wing and helped. He loved all the comedians he worked with and told me he would have loved to work with Steve Allen again. He was re-united with beautiful Gillian Lynne, they were special friends.

So TV programs and TV movies kept Tony busy and happy although his personal life was not going well.

"When you have been faced with death, there is no point living each day with doubt and unhappiness" — Anthony George Newley

Dear Tony,

I am so sorry about your marriage, but you have been through so much and maybe in time things will look better. I am glad you have a friend, but please do not rush in again with your eyes closed and make another mistake. She is very young, Tony, and you are not anymore! Just be careful, Darling. Please. It wouldn't be the worst thing in the world to be on your own for a little while.

You know you never bother me and I am always on the end of the phone. I hope you do come home and the show sounds wonderful although I do worry it may be too much for you.

Call me when you know what is happening. Of course the children love you, all of them, and things may still work out, Darling!

Remember those dreams, they are still there.

Goodbye Tony,

I love you,

Sue x

Chapter Seventeen

Someone Nice Like You

1989

Dear Tony,

I cannot control myself, thinking that in just a few weeks I will see you again. I wondered so many times if this day would come.

My family are all well and you will see them all soon. I look forward to meeting your daughter, too.

I know it will be hard for you, Darling, but you are strong and you have dealt with far worse.

I am selfish, Tony, but I am so glad you are coming home. See you soon.

I love you,

Sue x

I was so excited to be seeing Tony again, I had not seen him since he had been ill. I was invited on the Tony Blackburn Show on Capitol Radio to speak about *Stop The World*, as I had called in the previous week and seemed to know so much about Anthony Newley and the show. There was a quiz and I awarded tickets to four lucky contestants.

"Where was Anthony Newley born?" Tony Blackburn was shocked that so many people did not know who Anthony Newley was. He would be even more shocked today!

Tony sent me tickets for every matinée and evening of the *Stop the World* revival. I would have attended every performance if I could have managed it!

I even dragged my husband, who will always tell you he is not a Newley fan. I wonder why. My mother came on two occasions (Mum moved in with me when Dad died) and every other time, telling a little white lie, I would go on my own.

I loved the show and finally seeing Tony in the one show I had always wanted to see. Oh the music, that wonderful music. As expected Tony acted his socks off and although older was like a young boy on that stage.

Tony's mum and daughter were usually with him, but he always made time to say hello afterwards.

We had made plans to meet one evening just to catch up on old times. Tony had a reservation at the Savoy, a favourite of mine and we met after the show.

Tony, who was always proud of his physique, came to the door wrapped in a huge white toweling dressing gown. He looked tired and far older than he had just looked on the stage. He seemed small, and I don't even mean in stature. This man I had loved for all these years looked different, scared, and each line that I could clearly see on his face told a story. He was weary. He gave me one of his hugs and I thought I had broke a rib.

He was very sad. He told me about his marriage breakdown, and the tension that had caused with his family, and how at the ripe old age of 59 he had moved back in with Gracie.

When he went to dress, he tried to hide the scars from his surgery, and I ran to him and turned him around. He was still the beautiful man I remembered all those years ago and he had nothing to hide from me. I opened his robe. I gently, cautiously touched his scars. He closed his eyes and his hand cupped mine as I continued this delicate journey. He leaned into me and whispered into my neck

"We were always so comfortable together, weren't we?"

"We still are," I said and that night I fell asleep in his arms, as I had done so many times before.

The show was a minor success and did not run very long. There would be other wondeful shows to see Tony in now that he was home. Yes I was spoilt, as tickets were mine without asking.

Once Upon A Song was lovely, only to those who loved him.

Then there was *Scrooge,* wonderful *Scrooge.*

Tony played the Green Room, and although sick again, he gave a performance to equal any he gave on the Las Vegas stage. Some would say better. Every word he sang seemed more poignant and I cried through each performance.

Yes, my beautiful Tony was sick again.

Chapter Eighteen

The Last Song

Dear Tony,

It will be no good me telling you to slow down, you look so very tired.

Please be honest with people and tell them it is all getting too much, you have worked so hard all your life.

Would it be so hard for you to retire, Mr. Newley? Oh, forgive me I can only imagine your face when you read that!

When you are home I will pop over. SLOW DOWN, Newley!

I love you old boy,

Sue xx

Tony was presented with his *This Is Your Life* book in 1992 in Birmingham after one of his performances of *Scrooge*. I found it sad, as I didn't want to see his life discussed in a one-hour program, but it was lovely. All the people he so loved were there to talk about him, although there were a few of us missing. He was very tired, emotionally and physically, but he would talk about this day to me on more than one occasion.

"Can you believe they did this for me?"

"Yes. Darling, I can and no one was more deserving."

Tony had again met his old friend and love Gina, and they re-kindled the fire that started way back in the 50s. He finally had someone he felt really happy with and this truly made me happy, too.

"We came back together at the perfect time, I suppose…but it ended too soon." — Gina Fratini

Tony had also made up with his second wife, encouraged by his children to stop being so stubborn, and this also brought him comfort.

I went to see Tony many times in Esher, I still found it hard to see him back home living with his dear Mum. Even though she was now in her 90s, she would wait on her "boy" hand and foot.

"Look at all the 'Newley' stuff," he would say. There were boxes everywhere and I think he found it hard to make his mark on this home. "Look at Newley here."

"I'm looking at you," I would say, and would shrug.

His dressing room contained his clothes and shoes, and there were pictures of his loved ones, his Olbas oil placed stategically on his bedside cabinet. But if you didn't know Tony was there, you wouldn't have guessed. We rummaged through the boxes and I put things away for him.

"If you want anything," he would say, "Take it." He really was low.

I never really had fallen in love with Tony the star, but Tony the man. I hope you do not find that hard to believe.

Tony enjoyed the trappings being famous brought him, but being loved and held physically and emotionally gave him more than any award or trinket ever could.

Tony, the man who made us laugh, was confident, proud, and respected. Tony, the man I loved, was gentle, caring, generous, and kind.

"My Jewish Jeckyll and Hyde" is what I called him and he smiled that smile!

Yes I did take some things, some precious things he wanted to be thrown away; I could never have let that happen. I will cherish them always and my children have clear instructions what to do if anything should happen to me. 48 years of collecting, you can only imagine what I have!

Tony was getting ready to be interviewd by a young man named Paul he had met after *Stop the World*. He was not looking forward to it, but said he promised. I made him promise if it got to much he would tell them. I think the young interviewer many of you will know, our Paul Goodhead who runs The Newley Appreciation Society.

Scrooge opened to wonderful reviews in the West End and Tony nailed the role and very quickly it became his. I saw it so many times, and my children and yours can probably recall his performance till this day. His performances in *Scrooge* became less and less, and I cannot write without crying of the day I decided to take my daughter as a surprise to find he was not appearing.

I was invited to his home the following day. My visit to Esher brought some news I wasn't sure I could cope with, but knew I must. Tony and Gina were going to live in Florida. They were both sure that the heat would be better for Tony than remaining in the damp and cold of England. He would also be able to see his children easier and all in all this was the right thing for him to do.

Outside the Adelphi Theatre, 1997

From the 1989 revival of STOP THE WORLD — I WANT TO GET OFF

Dear Tony

Chapter Nineteen

The Party's Over

Having to let him go again was probably one of the most painful things I have ever had to endure in my life. We held each other for what seemed like an eternity, but those minutes, those precious minutes are etched in my heart.

"I don't want to die, I have so much I want to do" he said with tears running down his cheek

"Listen," I said, "you silly bugger, only the good die young. You'll be here for a long time yet."

"You know, in a few months nobody will even remember me."

"As long as I am breathing, Mr. Newley, you will never be forgotten, I promise you that, my love." I kissed him on the cheek.

Tony took my hand and led me outside, we sat drinking tea. He put a pillow from the chair on the lawn and knelt by my side. "I have to do this," he said with his voice cracking, "I need to be away from here and Gracie. I don't feel I am the man I should be when I'm here. I want to feel like me again, Flower. I was fun once, wasn't I? If my end is near, maybe that is one show I can get right. We were comfortable together."

"We still are," were the last face-to-face words I spoke to my old love.

I held him so tight and cried like I had done over him once before. We kissed and our lips seemed locked for ages. And this I swear to you with all my heart, will explain why I fell in love with Anthony Newley.

He turned me around and whispered "Go and don't turn around or I'll turn to salt." I was his Sara again for those few minutes.

I knew I would never see him again. We exchanged phone calls, and a few letters.

Dear Darling Tony,

I hope you are not feeling too bad. Is the treatment as ghastly as you expected? If any of us who love you could ease your pain you know we would. I feel so empty, so helpless.

Stay strong Tone, and when you are too tired to fight, make sure everyone knows.

I can still feel you in my heart, and if yours ever aches it is me just being the pain in the ass who always loved you so very much. Who still loves you so very much!

God Bless you, darling friend,

Sue xx

The calls stopped, and the letters became harder to read, he was finding it too difficult to write. He was so sick from the medicine. I had called Gina a few times to be told he was comfortable.

March

I never heard from Tony again. I spoke to Gina on March 22nd and was told they were doing what they could to ensure he was pain free.

April 14th 1999 8.35pm

Gina phoned and said Tony had died peacefully in her arms.

Part of me died that day too.

All the papers reported he was surrounded by all the women that he loved, Some of them, yes.

"Why would I forget someone who gave me so much to remember?" — Susan Jane Selfe

Chapter Twenty

Bye Bye Brown Eyes

My Darling Tony,

Now you have bloody upset me. How could you leave me with all I have done for you?

I listened to your stories of the other women and I stood by you when you married, knowing in my heart it was me you should have been with. I picked you up when you were down. I put the pieces back together when you were broke. You trusted me as I trusted you. I listened to your problems and always tried to find a solution, and knew you wouldn't listen anyway.

I was always here for you, I stayed here, even though you chose not to!
I loved you, when I should have been angry.
I loved you even when you never loved yourself.
I loved you when you broke my heart.
I loved you when you smiled and when you cried.
I loved you when you were happy, and even more when you were sad.
I love you Noobs and I will for the rest of my life.

TELL ME THE TRUTH ABOUT LOVE

When it comes will it come without warning
Just as I'm picking my nose?
Will it knock at my door in the morning
or tread in the bus on my toes?
Will it come like a change in the weather?
Will its greetings be courteous or rough?
Will it alter my life all forever?
Oh tell me the truth about love.

W. H. Auden

Goodbye Tony,

You know I love you,

Sue x

This was our favourite poem.

Dear Tony

Chapter Twenty One

No Such Thing as Love

This part of the story is very hard for me to write. You see I was a wife, mother, grandmother, and yet I grieved for this man I so loved. I could not let this affect my family life. I could not let my dear husband know how much I was hurting. He knew something was wrong, the constant tears, the mood swings. It did affect everything!

I lost my job. I couldn't concentrate, I couldn't care for other people if I could not care for myself.

I asked for counselling, and it was good to have someone to confide in, someone who would never judge me. I was racked with guilt, I hated what I had done, what I had become. Therapy did help me, it really helped! Not very long after Tony died, I trained to be a therapist myself. I felt like I had been doing it for years with him and I found it easy. I studied Carl Rogers and giving Unconditional Positive Regard was easy. I loved Tony and did this everyday with him, angry or not.

My mother was my saving grace, she loved Tony and I could talk to her.

I don't feel I need to write this, but I will. I love my husband, but could I discuss this with him? I think you all know the answer. Can you love more than one person at a time? I know that answer.

Dear Tony,

I sat and looked at all the beautiful things you have given me through the years, they shine and they sparkle, but not nearly as bright as you did, my darling.

Are you with Gracie? Are you sharing a nightly tipple? Are you at peace my beautiful friend?

I miss you. The days seem so long, and the nights not long enough. I shut my eyes, but sleep never comes. You rest, as now is the time you can.

I love you as much now as I did all those years ago. Thank you for giving me these memories.

Talk soon,

Sue xx

Dear Tony

Chapter Twenty Two

Me Without You

The Anthony Newley Appreciation Society. I knew it was there, but I couldn't join right away. I knew Paul, but it would take all my strength to finally make contact.

I remember after corresponding with Paul through email and phone calls, he told me he was coming to London and we would finally meet. I was so nervous, in my crazy head I wondered if Paul was like Tony. I could never work out why Paul was running the society; why didn't Tony tell me about this? He hated fan clubs so I was confused, but yet so excited. We were meeting in Covent Garden in London.

I came out of the train station and had a quick look around. I saw no Newley look-a-likes. I guess he wasn't there yet. I started to walk, it was so cold that day.

My phone bleeped with a message. "I'm here." Where? I walked back and looked down the line of anxious people waiting to be met.

The tall dark skinned man with the yellow suit was not him. The tall leggy blonde with red lipstick, definately was not him. The chap painted silver and doing the Michael Jackson moonwalk — please don't let it be him!

Then a man maybe slightly smaller than our Tony, but with a smile as big waved. We hugged and shared a kiss, I didn't know at that moment, but very soon after that, Paul would also play a big part in my life. We went to a lovely place we ate, drank wine, we laughed, and I cried.

Paul knew of me and I of him, and a friendship that might not have happened if we had not known Tony was made. We shared our love of Tony and so many wonderful stories. Paul shared all the wonderful things Tony had also given him. Paul is an entertainer and my family and I went to one of his shows. I presented Paul with a pair of Tony's cuff links for good luck. Paul and I became collaborators on projects and friends, too. We are so different in every aspect except the one that really counts our dear friend Tony.

You see, when you were really touched by Tony you become and act a certain way. He would enter your heart by a one way door, and once there would remain.

To this day I am grateful to have Paul in my life, and I think Tony would be glad too.

So I joined the Newley Society, started a Facebook page and try to fulfill the promise I made to Tony.

I began to let other people into my heart, rather than bottle everything up.

I guess I wondered how could anyone love him like I did? How could anybody appreciate him like I did? I never thought about his family or friends, or all of you that love and adore him. Why should I?

My best friend said I hope that writing this will help you heal, as love is not meant to hurt. All I know is that the pain I felt when he died, the pain I feel even now can be torture.

Oh yes, Mr. Newley, "Love Has The Longest Memory Of All"

Chapter Twenty Three

Remember Me

Dear Tony,

So I've written our story. I cut out the juicy bits and kept in the the sweet bits, as you were the sweetest man I have ever known.

How I loved to walk with you. The world looked different when I was with you. Trees were not just green, they were emerald. The sky a deep azure, and the sun hung in the sky above like the biggest yellow balloon

Each day was another to treasure. I waited to see what would come next. What would you say, what would you do? We had fun, didn't we?

We made each other laugh. Do you remember when you took me shopping and gave me something to hold, then so loud you said "Put that back, you must not steal!" Everybody looked at me and you burst out laughing.

Not everything you did made me laugh! I think of the times we would just sit in the back garden and turn over stones and watch the bugs that were underneath do their thing. All good until one came to near to you. Boy, could you move quick, Newley!

More than anything I think of you, the you I loved so. The crazy, funny, passionate, deep, thoughtful, spontaneous, loving joker who brightened my world and so many others. The man who made us laugh and cry.

I hope now you know how much you were loved, how much the people whose lives you touch miss you.

I thought about walking away once, just for a minute. I'm so glad I didn't.

I love you, Tony.

Sue xx

Let me tell you about Newley Night and how it came about.

I was speaking to a friend and I asked, "Don't people ever get together to celebrate Tony and his music?"

The response was "No! No one is interested anymore."

To me this was like showing a bull, a Brooklyn bull, a red flag. I went on my Newley Facebook page and asked the question, "Would anybody be interested in meeting me to celebrate the life of the greatest British entertainer that ever lived? We could talk about him, have a knees up and eat fish and chips and pie mash and liquor."

My Newley page lit up and within a couple of hours I had 50 replies. I had the greatest musicians sitting in a backstreet pub in West London. The Lord Nelson was my local and although at the time the young landlord was not over familiar with Tony, he helped me beyond the call of duty. He spent hours with me choosing the music, went to Hackney to collect the food, and when he left my home one night, I could hear him singing "D'Darling." I knew I had accomplished more than I could have imagined!

On April 14th 2012, we had a piano player who had played for Bowie playing by the men's bathroom! We had a top British actor who was due to open on the following day in the West End do a complete set. We had Newley magic. I will admit there was only 33 of us, but it was the start I wanted, that my darling friend was being honoured and loved. We sang till we could sing no more. I was beyond happy and the feedback was truly amazing.

This year, April 13th, we went upscale to Tony's Soho, Gerry's. It is the best place and I could see Tony coming down the stairs as I chose it. The same wonderful muscians, plus new faces and two idols of mine performed. The place was packed, standing room only. We sang, we brought the roof down, we laughed, we had made new friends. The following morning, Social networking sites were alive with Newley. and this old woman felt alive again!

Newley Night 3 is being planned as I write. Wonderful, talented people contact me and ask if they can sing. I can hear Tony say, "They want to do this for me?" Oh yes, Darling, they most certainly do!

Soon this will be a social event nobody will want to miss.

"Want to go on holiday?" "No, it's Newley Night!"

"Are you going to the match?" "No, it's Newley Night!"

"Want tickets to see Michael Buble?" "Who? No, it's Newley Night!"

Dear Tony

Newley Night is now here to stay!

Thank you,

Steve Furst
Clifford Slapper
David Boyle
Count Indigo
Jona Lewie
Phil Dirtbox
Robert Charles Walter Grindrod
Thank you all for your support and love.

Remember that night I told you about at the Savoy Hotel? Tony said to me that night, "Flower, I must have been such a bloody disappointment to you."

I said, "Only once in all these years did you ever disappoint me." He knew when that was. Forget you, why would anyone want to?

You know Tony, I made the right decision in Soho London on that warm summers night. I think I love you, yes, I'm sure that I do!

This Flower continues to bloom

84

Dear Tony

Thank You, Sweet Angel

Can you do me a favour, if it isn't too much,
I have something I really must say.
I need to tell my friend I love him, but my friend has gone away.

I need you to hug him and hold him so tight,
he could cope with the days, but not always the nights.

Can you tell him I smile and my tears are now dry,
and I'm dreaming of the sun, the moon, and the sky.

Can you tell him each moment he will be on my mind,
Thank you, Sweet Angel, you really are kind.

He was not very well, and he wanted to stay,
but it all got too much and he went on his way.

He was my world, a joy,
he was simply divine.
Thank you Sweet Angel
you really are kind

Susan Jane Selfe

September 2013